Also by David Sebra

The Yellow Baton

ISBN-9798362371128

Ten Teachings I Learned From Jesus

As Found In The New Testament

David Sebra

Contents

*****

Preface

While the Lord and Master, Jesus Christ, was in His earthly ministry He performed miracles, healed the sick, confounded the learned, gave solid direction to His apostles, and spoke in parables. Reading all of these accounts can be a spiritual "pick me up" and provide direction in our lives. We can draw closer to the Savior and become better committed to being His disciple.

So who am I to think that my top 10 list is any better than yours? It is not. I am simply a devoted Christian, just like you. If we compared our lists I am sure we would see common themes. I developed this list only to inspire a reader to follow Christ. I recommend you read the pertinent scripture first in its entirety, then read my commentary, and then re-read the scripture again. This will expand your understanding and commitment.

All scripture references continued herein are from the King James Version of the *Holy Bible*.

The Healing of Jairus' Daughter

Luke 8:40-56

Mark 5:21-43

The account of this experience is found in two places in the *New Testament.* One is in Mark 5:21-43, but I am using the version recorded by the apostle Luke. It comes on the heels of two mighty miracles. "Now it came to pass on a certain day, that he went into a ship with his disciples: and he said unto them, Let us go over unto the other side of the lake." (Luke 8:22) The lake that is referenced here is the Sea of Galilee. While on the journey upon the waters, the disciples fell asleep. Later they were awakened by a serious storm and they undoubtedly feared for their lives. Jesus simply rebuked the tempest, which gave new insight to His followers as to who He was.

Upon arrival on the eastern side of the Sea of Galilee the group make their way to the town of the home of the Gadarenes. Some *Bible* experts believe this to be the town of Gadara, but the exact location is unimportant. What happened there is important. This is where the Master performed the miracle of casting the evil spirits into a herd of swine and they ran off a cliff and perished. For His efforts, Jesus and His followers were told to get out of their town. One can only wonder what other blessings might have been bestowed upon those residents had they had a different spiritual mindset. So back they go to the ship and return to western side of the sea.

It seems that almost immediately the group was welcomed and a throng gathered around them. "And it came to pass, that, when Jesus was returned, the people *gladly* received him: for they were all waiting for him." (Luke 8:40) That is a much different reception from the one they experienced back in Gadara. A supplication from one in the crowd came right away.

"And, behold, there came a man named Jairus, and he was a ruler of the synagogue: and he fell down at Jesus' feet, and besought him that he would come into his house:

For he had one only daughter, about twelve years of age, and she lay a dying…." (versus 41-42)

This is probably a good place to pause and ponder this situation. Jairus was a powerful man and leader. Had he also been waiting there with the crowd for the return of the Master? Unlike the Gadarenes, his spiritual mindset was of faith and hope. And observe how this man of power approached Jesus. He fell at His feet! How could the compassionate Jesus refuse this request? He couldn't.

Now Jesus, Jairus, the disciples, and many others in the crowd proceeded to the home of the ruler. The end of verse 42 gives an important piece of information. ".... But as he went the people thronged him." All of us have probably been in a throng. Perhaps it was entering or leaving a sports venue or a cinema. There we move along bumping shoulders and constantly adjusting our speed so we don't step on the person in front of us. "Excuse me," is frequently heard. That is what Jesus was experiencing, but probably more intense. Isn't it easy to imagine how many in the throng wanted to touch Him? In fact, someone did.

"And a woman having an issue of blood twelve years, which had spent all her living upon physicians, neither could be healed of any,

Came behind *him,* and touched the border of his garment: and immediately her issue of blood stanched." (verses 43-44)

Like Jairus, this is another great demonstration of faith and hope. Her unhealed sore plagued her for twelve years. That is a very long time to maintain hope. She had spent all her earnings during that time seeking a cure, and found none. Her faith propelled this woman to weave through the crowd and get to where she could just touch Jesus' clothing. That's all she felt she needed to do. And it worked. Verse 44 states the issue was stanched, which means stopped.

This experience doesn't end there. It is doubtful that anyone in the throng knew what had happened, except one person. Apparently Jesus stopped and said, "….Who touched me?…" No one fessed up to it. Peter couldn't believe that Jesus could feel such a thing happening due to the crowd. "….Peter and they that were with him said, Master, the multitude throng thee and press *thee,* and sayest thou, Who touched me?" (verse 45) The next verse provides the authoritative reply. "And Jesus said, Somebody hath touched me: for I perceive that virtue is gone out of me."

All eyes are now watching this exchange. Look at the attitude of the woman in verse 47. "And when the woman saw that she was not hid, she came trembling, and falling down before him, she declared unto him before all the people for what cause she had touched him and how she was healed immediately." Just as Jairus did, she fell to Jesus' feet. Her reward for her faith and hope went much further than the stopping of the blood. "And he said unto her, Daughter, be of good comfort: thy faith hath made thee whole; go in peace." (verse 48) She could indeed depart in peace and that is very instructive to all of us.

We do not know how long this interchange lasted but it interrupted something important. Remember that Jesus was on the way to heal Jairus' daughter. There is a great message in this scenario. While on an errand of significance and importance, Jesus took the time to tend to the needs of another person.

I will relate a personal experience that applies what I learned from this account. One day I was driving to meet up with the Stake Relief Society Presidency to assist them in a service project. On the left side of the street I saw a woman on the sidewalk. It looked like she had fallen and when she saw my car she waved her hand to get my attention. Her face looked distressed. Even though I was on my way to render service I stopped to help this woman. She explained she was from out of the area and her son had abandoned her there. She didn't speak English very well as she was Hispanic and I don't speak Spanish. I helped her into my car and I took to a firehouse nearby. There was someone there who spoke Spanish and they took her in and tended to her needs. I then proceeded on my way to complete my other service. The lesson I learned is to never be in a rush, even while on the Lord's errand, so the spirit can't reach you and give you additional direction.

But we are not done learning from this beautiful experience as told by Luke. As Jairus was watching these events unfold, he must have felt really good inside that he has come to the right person in his time of need. Anticipation that Jesus' healing powers will also extend to his daughter would be high. Just as the Lord was telling the woman to "go in peace", one of the servants of Jairus arrived on the scene with a dire message. ".... Thy daughter is dead; trouble not the Master." (Verse 49) Jairus' heart must have plummeted.

I can picture Jesus and Jairus locking eyes onto each other. Now listen to the beautiful teaching Jesus gave to Jairus in verse 50. "But when Jesus heard *it,* he answered him, saying, **Fear not: believe only**, and she shall be made whole." [my emphasis added] Compassion will be forthcoming but Jairus must extend his faith a little more, in fact, a lot more. For now his daughter has passed. "Fear not; believe only." Obviously I have never gone through this same type of Jairus experience but I have been brought to the brink of situations where I needed to fear not. When we do not give in to fear but fully believe, the blessings of heaven are poured down. That is exactly what happened to Jairus. That is exactly what happened to the woman. Let's read the rest of Luke's words.

"51 And when he came into the house, he suffered no man to go in, save Peter, and James, and John, and the father and the mother of the maiden.

52 And all wept, and bewailed her: but he said, Weep not; she is not dead, but sleepeth.

53 And they laughed him to scorn, knowing that she was dead.

54 And he put them all out, and took her by the hand, and called, saying, Maid, arise.

55 And her spirit came again, and she arose straightway: and he commanded to give her meat.

56 And her parents were astonished: but he charged them that they should tell no man what was done."

Notice that this was not a matter of fact recitation. It was a sacred experience for a limited group of people. The throng was kept outside the home. The others who were already in the house were doubtful that the sting of death could be reversed. They scorned the Lord when He suggested the little girl only slept. Their scorn became cause for their ejection of the sacred scene. It was not a punishment, but a special occasion as this turned out to be, should have only faithful believers present. It is hard for me to find fault with the unbelievers, for bringing a person back from death was not a common event then or today. There is no definitive chronology in the *New Testament*, but Luke tells of the raising of a son of a widow in the city of Nain in his previous chapter. We have no idea if the mourners knew of the event at Nain. Certainly the servant that bore the news to Jairus of the death of his daughter felt there was no value in bringing Christ to the lamenting home. The raising of Jesus' close friend, Lazarus, apparently occurred afterward. And this brings us to the summation of this lesson. The act of not fearing can propel us to greater heights and blessings.

The Return of the Prodigal Son

Luke 15:11–32

In the fifteenth chapter of Luke he relates a trilogy of parables that may seem to be duplicative of each other, but a closer inspection reveals some slight differences. They are known as the parables of the Lost Sheep, the Piece of Silver, and the Prodigal Son. The situation of the lost sheep is that the sheep strayed without intending to get lost. This is kind of like a person slowly losing their testimony of Jesus Christ. The lost coin disappeared due to carelessness or neglect of others. Finally, the lost (or prodigal) son was through his own willful disobedience. That is not a good situation. I believe any of us can fall into either category from time to time. Resolution and returning to the fold differs slightly in each case. The last situation touches me the most.

Have any of you had a young child that decided to run away from home? Did they get very far? Perhaps they sat at the park two blocks away from home and after eating their scanty meal they brought with them, the decision is made to return. Fortunately at some point the child realizes that running away is not the answer. These little occurrences are sometimes cute and comical - after the fact. But sometimes they become gut wrenching and heart breaking. Such events require much attention and support from others. Often the estrangement lasts a very long time and there is nothing cute or comical about it. I believe the Savior gave us this parable to help us pull through such extreme pain. Let's read about one man's plight from Luke 15. Bear in mind that Luke is quoting Jesus as He tells this parable.

"11 And he said, A certain man had two sons:

12 And the younger of them said to his father, Father, give me the portion of goods that falleth to me. And he divided unto them his living.

13 And not many days after the younger son gathered all together, and took his journey into a far country, and there wasted his substance with riotous living."

We are not told the age of this young man nor what prompted his desire to leave home. Was he tired of being a farmer? That is not always an easy life. Perhaps there was jealousy between him and his brother. Jealously can be a powerful stimulus. Anciently, the older brother did seem to get preferential treatment. There is no statement of an argument with his parents. Whatever the reason, the young man decided to run away from home.

And run away he did! He didn't stop at the local park and eat his lunch. He went to a far country. Why? Nearby neighbors, friends, or relatives were not an option to him. He wanted to be far from the influence of his father. He wanted to be at a place where his father could not find him or try to bring him home. The desire to be on our own and make or own decisions without the experience of one who can help us, ofter brings disastrous results. It certainly did here. Wasting resources and embracing a debaucherous life style are certainly examples of inexperienced choice making. As expected, stark reality soon set in. .

"14 And when he had spent all, there arose a mighty famine in that land; and he began to be in want.

15 And he went and joined himself to a citizen of that country; and he sent him into his fields to feed swine.

16 And he would fain have filled his belly with the husks that the swine did eat: and no man gave unto him."

The folly of youth normally doesn't plan for the future nor consider what can happen if things go awry. He has spent all his money and is far from a familiar support system (loving parents) that can help him. The friends he probably thought he was making with his new life style no longer had use for him. He is alone and destitute. That is an awful feeling. It can apply to us in spiritual, economic, or simple daily life situations.

Being in that circumstance has few viable options. The young man had to find a job to survive. What did he select? A pig farmer! Knowing of the Israelite animosity toward swine, made this choice even more reprehensible. But it was all he had and even that wasn't sufficient.

I love the teaching that the Christ said next in verse 17. "And when he came to himself…." This is a very introspective statement that implies that the young man had a good talk with himself. He pondered in his mind what he had done, and how he can rectify his woeful life. Fortunately he came to the proper conclusion: "It is time to go home." It seems that we also need to apply this "coming to ourselves" process in our lives repeatedly as the situation dictates. This requires a transformation from pitting our will against God's (or against a parent, spouse, or another person) to accepting the will of a wise and kind being.

Humility is the key and the next two verses clearly demonstrate that the young man is now humble.

"18 I will arise and go to my father, and will say unto him, Father, I have sinned against heaven, and before thee,

19 And am no more worthy to be called thy son: make me as one of thy hired servants."

As Jesus continues the story, a beautiful scene develops. I envision an elderly man, whose aging has been accelerated by the absence of his son. Perhaps he is sitting out front of his house at the end of the day, gazing out to the horizon. The father does this frequently and there is hope that one day they will be reunited. Prayers are probably often offered to that effect. The day finally comes!

"20 And he arose, and came to his father. But when he was yet a great way off, his father saw him, and had compassion, and ran, and fell on his neck, and kissed him."

What a joyful reunion this was. I have not personally experienced this, but I have had the pleasure of meeting an old friend after years of no contact. Hearty handshakes and thunderous back slaps abounded as the reacquaintance occurred. This must be similar, if only in a small way, to what the man and his young son felt. But however joyful the son was, he still felt underserving to be in his father's presence.

"21 And the son said unto him, Father, I have sinned against heaven, and in thy sight, and am no more worthy to be called thy son."

That is a natural attitude to have. The son didn't know what to expect when he returned home. Will he be allowed to stay? Will punishment be doled out? Most importantly, will he be accepted? That was all cleared up in the father's actions.

"22 But the father said to his servants, Bring forth the best robe, and put it on him; and put a ring on his hand, and shoes on his feet:

23 And bring hither the fatted calf, and kill it; and let us eat, and be merry:

24 For this my son was dead, and is alive again; he was lost, and is found. And they began to be merry."

The son's doubts and fears are evaporated into the air by his father's compassionate and sincere words.

Why do I love this parable? It is fully rich with symbolism of our relationship with our Father and our Savior. We come to this earth and spend a few decades and then depart. What occurs during this earthy time is of extreme importance and the power of the atonement of Jesus Christ can help us return "to our home".

I know many people who do a very good job of managing their earthly time. Being friends with such individuals helps me to improve myself as they are good examples to follow. But what happens when we stray off the path? It doesn't matter if we go away to a far country for unbecoming behavior, or just a couple of steps away. Heavenly Father will **always** be waiting for us, to accept us back home. A repentant soul is always welcomed back. It can never be too late to return. We just sometimes need to “come to ourselves”.

The Good Samaritan

Luke 10:25-37

This parable has become an all time favorite of both Christian and non-Christian people throughout the world for centuries. Indeed, it takes its rightful stature due to its basic and important theme - helping mankind in need. Relief efforts are still ongoing in the world today with many of us trying to alleviate, even in a small way, part of the tremendous desperation that exists in so many parts of the world. There are even organizations that have adopted the parable's title in their names.

Let's go to Luke chapter 10 and absorb the meaning of this teaching. But first, some background from chapter 9 will be helpful. The occasion of his teaching was shortly after the marvelous event that took place on the Mount of Transfiguration, (possibly Mount Hermon). After descending from the hill a crowd gathered around Jesus and his disciples. Miracles were performed and much instruction was given to the Twelve. The time had now come for the Master to go to Jerusalem and Jesus and the others would have to continue their travels through Samaria to get to their destination. Messengers were sent in advance of His journey to a village in Samaria to make preparations for His coming. However, the villagers there did not publicly receive Jesus for they knew He was headed to Jerusalem. There was great animosity between Samaria and Israel. Jesus skillfully used this known antipathy as a key feature in His parable.

After arriving in Jerusalem, we are not told where they gathered, but Luke tells us that Jesus took some time and offered His thanks to the Father for the apostles and the wisdom they were gaining. He even told them privately that they were blessed for what they are able to witness. At one point a man decides to ask Him a question. When we ask a question of Deity we should be prepared for the answer. Often we are not. That is sometimes the case with me and it certainly was for this person who was described as a lawyer. Let's examine the dialogue between the lawyer and the Savior.

"25 And, behold, a certain lawyer stood up, and tempted him, saying, Master, what shall I do to inherit eternal life?"

OK, the first observation is that the man was tempting Christ. He wanted to find some way to trip Him up with His words. That is not possible. The man wasn't seeking knowledge but attempting to lay a snare. Actually, the question that is asked is a very good one, if the person is sincere. In fact, we should ourselves constantly be asking the Father this very question. And then be prepared and committed to accept and follow the answer.

"26 He said unto him, What is written in the law? how readest thou?

27 And he answering said, Thou shalt love the Lord thy God with all thy heart, and with all thy soul, and with all thy strength, and with all thy mind; and thy neighbour as thyself."

This person was knowable enough to know some of the Hebrew law. He has really answered his own question, but he didn't see that. I can imagine a couple of the apostles grinning, knowing how this is going to turn out.

Jesus continues. "28 And he said unto him, Thou hast answered right: this do, and thou shalt live."

II is time for the man to quit, for a proper and introspective answer has been given. But remember, the lawyer was looking for an unfair advantage, not spiritual enlightenment. So he pressed further.

"29 But he, willing to justify himself, said unto Jesus, And who is my neighbor?"

I'm actually grateful for this discussion for it reveals to me some majestic and heavenly doctrine. It provides me teachings that I need to fully embrace in my life to be a true Christian. Now comes the parable.

“30 And Jesus answering said, A certain man went down from Jerusalem to Jericho, and fell among thieves, which stripped him of his raiment, and wounded him, and departed, leaving him half dead.”

Apparently the road to Jericho had a bad reputation for travelers back then and was not a place for a person traveling alone.

“31 And by chance there came down a certain priest that way: and when he saw him, he passed by on the other side.

32 And likewise a Levite, when he was at the place, came and looked on him, and passed by on the other side.”

These passersby were carefully chosen for the parable. Instead of simply saying a man or a woman passed by, He selected two people that were highly influential and respected at that time. The priests served as interceders between the Hebrew people and their god. They performed their duties in the temple with various rites and sacrifices. Priests were required to be of the tribe of Levi, hence a Levite. So, the expectation of these two persons is they would always do the right thing and care for their flock in any required manner. When the priest saw the injured man from far away, he crossed to the other side of the road so he didn’t have to get involved. The Levite actually came up close to the injured one and then likewise went around him. Now consider the irony in the next verse.

"33 But a certain Samaritan, as he journeyed, came where he was: and when he saw him, he had compassion on him,"

Remember the enmity that the Samaritans had for Israel? Surely such a person would not stop and help an Israelite. But he did!

"34 And went to him, and bound up his wounds, pouring in oil and wine, and set him on his own beast, and brought him to an inn, and took care of him.

35 And on the morrow when he departed, he took out two pence, and gave them to the host, and said unto him, Take care of him; and whatsoever thou spendest more, when I come again, I will repay thee."

The Samaritan went the extra mile in caring for this victimized soul. Which is what the priest and Levite should have done. This is a great example to us. Jesus ties the story up nicely by addressing the lawyer. "36 Which now of these three, thinkest thou, was neighbour unto him that fell among the thieves?"

The trap was avoided and the man had no choice but to answer, "37 And he said, He that shewed mercy on him…." To which Christ replied, "….Then said Jesus unto him, Go, and do thou likewise."

Understanding this Messianic teaching is fairly easy, but its application to us personally can be a huge challenge. The cry for help can be for physical, mental, financial, or spiritual needs. When these opportunities cross our way, so do doubts and obstacles.

"It's none of my business." or

"I don't have the time." or

"Someone else can do it better." or

"It's their own fault. Let them get out of their own mess." or

"I don't know how." or

"I don't have the resources." or

"They are just trying to take advantage of my generosity."

I will close this chapter with a personal story of how I applied this teaching in my life. One time I was on a road trip with my three adult sons to attend a college football game. We decided to share expenses in an equitable way. Each of us paid our own airfare and game tickets. I paid for the hotel room. One son took care of the car rental and another would pay for meals. After settling in to our hotel room we decided to go purchase snacks. A grocery store was nearby so we went there. At the checkout area as a son was ready to pay for the goodies, the clerk asked him if he wanted cash back. My son replied, "Yes" and received what he asked for.

We went back to our car and as we were leaving the parking lot, there was a man sitting on the ground with some sort of a sign requesting help. He was a pleasant looking and clean cut gentleman. We drove out onto the street and about a half a block away, we all in unison said, “Wait! We have to go back and help the man.” We went back into the parking lot and stopped and all of us pulled put of our pockets all the cash we had. It was given to one of my boys who walked over and gave it to the destitute person. A grateful and sincere “Thank you,” was given by the man. Then we went on our way. There is an interesting twist to this story. Driving back to our hotel, the son who got the cash at the grocery store checkout said, “I never get cash back when I purchase items. This time I felt prompted to do so.”

And so it goes. When we accept the role of the Samaritan, the Lord provides the way for us to overcome any obstacle to serve His people.

The Rich Young Man

Matthew 19:16-24

Mark 10:17-31

Luke 18:18-30

This next teaching I gained may have been the hardest for me to apply, and actually, still is. Jesus had been teaching in Galilee and departed for the coast of Judea. As has become the norm, large groups of people are following Him and the apostles. Often, as we saw in the previous chapter, there were many in the crowd who were seeking to find fault and accusation with the Christ. Matthew Chapter 19 describes such a case. A group of Pharisees began to question Him one day regarding marriage and divorcement. That issue was put to bed, at least in the mind of the Savior. Then a touching scene is described by the former tax collector. Little children were then brought to the Savior and He blessed them. The group then went on their way.

The next teaching is introduced in this manner. “16 And, behold, one came and said unto him, Good Master, what good thing shall I do, that I may have eternal life?” Mark adds additional information about this encounter. “….there came one running, and kneeled to him….” (Mark 10:17) We are not told what prompted this young man with an important question. Perhaps he was present at the Sermon on the Mount wherein the command was given, “Be ye therefore perfect, even as your Father which is in heaven is perfect.” (Matt 5:48) Or maybe he heard about this new bold teaching from someone else. Certainly, the word of Jesus’ teachings were spreading. Another possible motive exists. In Luke 18:18 wherein it states, “And a certain ruler asked him….” The man was young and rich and also a ruler. He may have felt that he had it all, but yet, something was missing in his life By his own admission he had led an obedient spiritual life.

Whatever the reason, he wants to know how to receive eternal life. Don’t we all have similar thoughts? Aren’t we concerned if we are on the right path back to our Heavenly Father? This is an excellent pondering question to have throughout our lives and the perfection command a very intimidating standard. It would be good for us to remember that God does not ask anything of us that is not possible for us to obtain. He has proven that many times in the scriptures.

Here is Jesus' reply. "17 And he said unto him, Why callest thou me good? there is none good but one, that is, God: but if thou wilt enter into life, keep the commandments." The man wants to make sure he hasn't missed something in his life. "18 He saith unto him, Which?…." At that point the Lord recites to him most of the Ten Commandments. These are the same laws given to the ancient prophet, Moses, and has been a cornerstone in Israelite culture and theology ever since.

The nagging thoughts in his mind produced one of the most important questions for all mankind for all ages. "20 The young man saith unto him, All these things have I kept from my youth up: **what lack I yet?**" [my emphasis added] When we ask such a question of God, we must be prepared to be obedient to the answer. The response will be different for each of us because we are all individuals with unique characters. Here is what the rich young ruler was told.

"21 Jesus said unto him, If thou wilt be perfect, go and sell that thou hast, and give to the poor, and thou shalt have treasure in heaven: and come and follow me."

How ecstatic the man should have been. The Savior of us all just gave him the key to obtain eternal life. But that key has only the rich young ruler's name on it. The key that bears our name will look different. However, his reaction was non expectant. "22 But when the young man heard that saying, he went away sorrowful: for he had great possessions."

While watching the man walk away from eternity He said, "23 Then said Jesus unto his disciples, Verily I say unto you, That a rich man shall hardly enter into the kingdom of heaven.

24 And again I say unto you, It is easier for a camel to go through the eye of a needle, [speaking metaphorically] than for a rich man to enter into the kingdom of God."

I wish to relate a story to inspire us to understand the importance of seeking what holds us back from eternity. It is a beautiful story of a faithful pioneer woman, Drusilla Hendricks. (Gerald Lund, *Selected Writings Of Gerald N. Lund*, p321, 1999, © Gerald Lund, Used by Permission of Deseret Book Company.)

> Here is another example from the life of Drusilla Hendricks, who had given so much effort to care for a crippled husband. When they reached Winter Quarters in July 1846, her oldest boy, William, aged sixteen, was able to drive the team. She finally had a child old enough and strong enough to help with her husband and her children.

Then Captain James Allen from the United States Army rode into camp and said, "We're looking for five hundred volunteers for the Mormon Battalion," and young William Hendricks said, "Mother, I want to go." Not surprisingly, she said she didn't want him to go. She had already sent one man to war, and he had come back crippled. She adamantly refused to give in until the morning of the mustering when the men were preparing to march out. I would like to share with you from her own journal what happened. She said, "I went to get some flour from the wagon, and as I stood on the tongue the whispering of the Spirit said to me, 'Do you not want the greatest glory?' I answered in my natural voice, I was so surprised. 'Why, of course.' 'Then how can you get it without making the greatest sacrifice?'"

Many of us at that point would try to remind the Lord: Don't you remember what's been going on these last six years with me? But she said, in effect, "Lord, what lack I yet?" And then the Spirit whispered, "Let your son go in the Mormon

Battalion." So she returned to camp. William looked at her and said, "Mother, can I go?" And she said, "Yes." And then, weeping because she couldn't bear the thoughts of losing her son, she went about her duties. Her journal records, "I went to milk the cows. I thought they would shelter me in my tears. I knelt down and told the Lord if he wanted my child to take him, but I begged him that he would spare his life. Then a voice, that same spiritual voice that spoke to me before answered me saying, 'Drusilla, it shall be done unto you as it was unto Abraham when he offered Isaac on the altar.'" And then she concluded her account: "I don't know whether I milked or not, for all I felt was the presence of the Lord."

What a great blessing this woman received from asking “What lack I yet?” Let us ponder our lives and ask the same question and then have the courage to accept the Savior’s reply, and not walk away sorrowfully. And then, do it again, and again, and again.

The Command: To Judge Not

Matthew 7:1-5

The seventh chapter of Matthew concludes His narrative of the marvelous and voluminous set of Jesus' teachings that Christians call the Sermon on the Mount. This lengthy discourse also contains the Beatitudes ("blessed are ….") and was delivered on a hillside near the Sea of Galilee. This was a set of laws that fulfilled the ones He gave to Moses many centuries ago in Sinai. It became the higher law and has stayed in force to this day. So special is this sermon that a church has been erected on the perceived site. Almost every one of the 111 verses of the Sermon is a rich doctrinal statement. The text for this holy teaching that I have embraced is only 5 verses at the beginning of Matthew 7.

"1 Judge not, that ye be not judged.

2 For with what judgment ye judge, ye shall be judged: and with what measure ye mete, it shall be measured to you again.

3 And why beholdest thou the mote that is in thy brother's eye, but considerest not the beam that is in thine own eye?

4 Or how wilt thou say to thy brother, Let me pull out the mote out of thine eye; and, behold, a beam is in thine own eye?

5 Thou hypocrite, first cast out the beam out of thine own eye; and then shalt thou see clearly to cast out the mote out of thy brother's eye."

There are a lot of clichés that come to mind pertaining to judging others or situations. "Don't judge a book by it's cover." "People who live in glass houses should not throw stones." Verse 1 is frequently used as a retort in an argument to defend a position. The person saying it usually attempts to do so with authoritative finality. It is meant to shut down further discussion and that is very unfortunate because it may lead to severe misunderstandings and resentments. But does this verse from Jesus really mean not to have assessments or evaluations? How can we make proper choices unless we judge?

Often it helps to cross reference scripture verses to attain better context and comprehension. In helping to ascertain Jesus' real intent in Matthew 7, let's read another one of his sayings that is quoted by John. "Judge not according to the appearance, but judge righteous judgment." (John 7:24) This counsel advises us not to have superficial judgment. This is further supported by the example cited by Luke in chapter 7: 36-50. A pharisee invited the Lord to eat with him at his house. Upon sitting down to eat, a woman came in from outside and began washing Jesus' feet. The pharisee immediately judged the woman and described her as a sinner. His judgment was based upon her appearance and her lifestyle. He felt very strongly she should not be amongst them at the dinner table.

The pharisee was named Peter (not be confused with the apostle Simon Peter). The Master severely rebuked Peter and related to the group assembled there the parable of the debtors. This parable's meaning clearly points out that despite the woman's sins, she should be treated fairly and not be despised nor cast out. And this illustrates an important principle of the skill of judging situations. Judge the act and not the person. We can condemn the sin, but don't become "judge, juror, and executioner". When we step over that line we no longer are extending to the person a welcome hand to help them overcome the issue. Judging and casting out is not a remedial action. The principle of forgiveness taught by Christ ("forgive seventy times seven") is paramount in judgments.

Another aspect of wrongful judging is when we pre-judge. When we do that we become prejudiced. The sound of that word sends chills up the spine. No one wants to be guilty of being prejudiced. But when we judge by appearances only and pre judge without gaining pertinent facts, that is exactly what we do. We should always be in the mode of careful evaluation with accurate information. That will lead us to effective decision making.

Many years ago I had the opportunity to apply this teaching in my life. While attending college my wife and I went to church one morning. It was the first time for us with that congregation and we actually arrived a tad late so we sat in the back. During the meeting my scanners were searching the other parishioners and mentally to myself making judgments. “Who would be someone cool to hang out with?” I homed in on one man in particular. He had long hair, a mustache, and did not wear a tie. I’m very straight laced and proper. (Is that a quality or a fault?) So I was convinced that this person was someone I would not be comfortable with. That was that. I evaluated and judged and made my decision. Immediately after the conclusion of the services, this man made a bee-line to us and became the first person to introduce himself and sincerely welcomed us to church. We became good friends.

The Bold Declaration

Matthew 16:13-19

Mark 8:27-29

At one point during His ministry, Jesus and His disciples were traveling along the sea coast of a town called Cæsarea Philippi, This ancient city was located near the base of Mount Hermon, the possible site of the Mount of Transfiguration. It is now a national park in Israel. Picture if you will, this holy assemblage of men walking along the shore of the water. The Master stops and turns to His disciples and asks a question that should require some pondering before answering.

"13 When Jesus came into the coasts of Cæsarea Philippi, he asked his disciples, saying, Whom do men say that I the Son of man am?"

In today's vernacular Jesus is enquiring what the "word on the street" is about Him. The apostles spent time with their families and associated with others in the villages, so they would certainly hear what was being said. I am curious if He asked this question because that is what He wanted to know, or was there a deeper purpose. The dialogue continues.

"14 And they said, Some say that thou art John the Baptist: some, Elias; and others, Jeremias, or one of the prophets."

The rumors in the towns seemed to be rooted in superstition of great men returning from the dead. They don't understand it yet, but resurrection could not occur until the First-Fruit From The Grave comes forth. That leads Jesus to ask the all important and very personal question.

"15 He saith unto them, But whom say **ye** that I am?" [The highlighted emphasis is mine.]

Place yourself in that scene and remember you have traveled with the Lord and have seen and have absorbed also what the disciples witnessed and felt. What would be your answer? Would it be simple or complex? Would there be apprehension in your thoughts? Or would the answer be bold and declarative? The first apostle to speak at this moment was Peter. Many have speculated that Peter's Impetuous personality triggers this quick response. I disagree with that analysis.

"16 And Simon Peter answered and said, Thou art the Christ, the Son of the living God."

There it is - the bold declaration!

Many years ago I was speaking with a small. group of people concerning religion and one of the men in the group asked me a similar question as the disciples were asked. “Who do you believe Jesus Christ to be?” Well, my reply was impetuous. I said, “He is the Son of God.” Now that certainly is a correct answer, but it could have been much more meaningful. His next question was truly humbling to me. “Is that all?” Of course I had more to give but in replying too quickly, I missed the opportunity to make a bold declaration on who I really felt the Christ to be, as Peter did two millennia ago. I learned from that experience and aided by this doctrine and teaching moment of the Savior. I give much better answers now.

Peter’s answer to his Master revealed to Jesus what was in the heart of Peter. It wasn’t intellectual knowledge nor hearsay. It was a deeply rooted testimony of the divinity of the Savior. The Lord expressed his pleasure to Peter with this. “17 And Jesus answered and said unto him, Blessed art thou, Simon Barj-ona: for flesh and blood hath not revealed it unto thee, but my Father which is in heaven.” Then lofty and yet to be earned blessings were pronounced.

"18 And I say also unto thee, That thou art Peter, and upon this rock I will build my church; and the gates of hell shall not prevail against it.

"19 And I will give unto thee the keys of the kingdom of heaven: and whatsoever thou shalt bind on earth shall be bound in heaven: and whatsoever thou shalt loose on earth shall be loosed in heaven."

As I ponder what I have learned from this teaching of my Lord, I recall the enlightenment of another person. The man's name is Dietrich Bonhoeffer. Mr. Bonhoeffer was a Lutheran minster and lived in Germany during the World War II era. He was part of the resistance movement against the Nazi government and gave his life for his beliefs and actions. But a great teaching of his lived on. Dietrich felt peaching the word of God was a serious undertaking and he employed it with vigor. In 1932 he spoke at Finkenwalde Seminary (the Pomerania region in Germany) and said, "We must be able to speak about our faith so that hands will be stretched out toward us faster than we can fill them....Do not defend God's Word, but testify to it...." (Taken from *Bonhoeffer, Pastor, Martyr, Prophet, Spy,* by Eric Metaxas, Copyright © 2010 by Eric Metaxas. Used by permission of HarperCollins Christian Publishing. www.harpercollinschristian.com)

Follow the encouragement of Bonhoeffer and the example of Peter: declare your testimony of the Lord Jesus Christ with boldness.

The Ten Virgins

Matthew 25:1-13

Toward the end of the book of Matthew there are many chapters that deal with our personal relationship with God. If possible, if one reads 21 through 25 in a single setting, that can tie a lot of doctrine together and provide good context. I especially recommend reading chapters 24 and 25 together as though they were one chapter, for they are so closely related on the same subject. And that subject is the Savior's Second Coming. It is easy to fall into the trap to believe that since this event has been talked about for a couple of thousand of years and it is still not here, is it really going to happen? God has not revealed the exact time to us, but there are ample scriptures to help us look for that day and how to prepare for it. That preparation should be both individualistic and as a Christian community.

The Parable of the Ten Virgins is one that has been especially helpful to me to maintain my focus in my service to my Father in Heaven. There are two other names that have been associated with this parable: Parable of the Wise and Foolish Virgins and Parable of the Ten Bridesmaids. it is found only in Matthew 25:1-13.

The background that leads up to this parable is very noteworthy. Jesus, His apostles, and many followers are heading to Jerusalem for what will become known as His triumphal entry. A little east of the city of Jerusalem there is a hill of 2700 feet that provides a beautiful view of the Holy City. It is named the Mount of Olives, nicknamed Mount Olivet. The name comes from the obvious - it was covered with olive trees anciently. That tree's fruit was an important crop for Israel. When the entourage approaches Jerusalem they stop at Bethphage, a town at the base of Olivet. Two disciples are sent by Jesus to locate an ass and a colt. These animals would become the ones as prophesied by Zechariah to bring the Messiah into the city (Zechariah 9:9). This manner of entry through the main gates of a city was symbolic of the entry of a king.

This regal entry had the intended effect: "….all the city was moved, saying, Who is this?" (Matthew 21:10) He made His way to the temple where he proceeded to perform the well known cleansing by ridding the area of the tables and stalls of mammon. Healings were also performed and the spiritually minded people rejoiced, but

Jesus made few friends with the leadership of the people. That evening found Jesus and the group lodging at the town of Bethany, the same city where His dear friends Lazarus, Mary, ad Martha lived.

The next day Jesus returns to the temple to continue His teachings including the usage of parables. Further enemies were made as the Pharisees were condemned for their decayed state. Equal results occurred with His interaction with the Sadducees. There was much discussion in Jerusalem that centered on the end of the world and the sign of His coming. After his work was completed there, Christ left the temple and departed the city. They arrived at the Mount of Olives and they settled in at the mount and the Olivet Discourse begins at Matthew 24:3. "And as he sat upon the mount of Olives, the disciples came unto him privately, saying, Tell us, when shall these things be? and what shall be the sign of thy coming, and of the end of the world?"

It appears that only the Twelve Apostles are now with Jesus for this set of sermons. The remaining part of Matthew 24 is one of detailed explanations from Christ. Calamities that will proceed His Second Coming are told and the Parable of the Fig Tree is given. A person would be wise to study this chapter carefully and evaluate how these teachings compare to our present day conditions. Then in chapter 25, three parables to help us prepare for the Second Coming are given. The great teaching parable that so effected me, does so because it deals with our personal righteousness. It begins with Matthew 25:1.

"1 Then shall the kingdom of heaven be likened unto ten virgins, which took their lamps, and went forth to meet the bridegroom."

It is universally accepted in the Christian community that the virgins are symbolic of Christ's church members. Another way of viewing their role is that they are torchbearers or bridesmaids. The bridegroom represents the Lord Jesus Christ. In ancient Jewish weddings, they actually began with the betrothal which could be as much as a year prior. It is a firm commitment to marriage but does not get finalized until the wedding ceremony. The exact day and time pf the ceremony is not set, but is decided by the groom's father. So the virgins or bridesmaids must stand watch and always be prepared for when the hour is come. The symbolism is very strong as we are to watch for the Second Coming, not knowing the hour and we must be prepared to meet Him.

Continuing in the parable, "2 And five of them were wise, and five were foolish.

3 They that were foolish took their lamps, and took no oil with them:

4 But the wise took oil in their vessels with their lamps."

A couple points come to my mind. The first one is promoted by His teachings in the previous chapter. “Then shall two be in the field; the one shall be taken, and the other left.” (Matthew 24:40) As much as we would like all of our family and our friends and neighbors to be present at that grand day, the reality of the situation is that all will not be there. We shouldn’t be caught up with a set percentage as the teachings indicate (50%), but know we have serious and sacred work to do to achieve as high a number as possible.

Secondly, the distinguishing characteristic between the wise and foolish virgins is not related to intelligence, wealth, position, nor opportunity. Rather, it is solely based on preparation, our own personal preparation. Regardless of our station in life, whether high or low or in between, we can prepare for the day of the coming of the Bridegroom with whatever means we have. If we do our best, it will be fully accepted of the Lord. Isn’t that wonderful to know? We do our best and that’s good enough for Him.

Next, we see a real life situation staring at us. “5 While the bridegroom tarried, they all slumbered and slept.” It was taking a long time for the bridegroom to arrive, so all he virgins slept. It has been a long time since these prophecies were given. Are we sleeping? The condemnation was not bestowed upon the foolish virgins for sleeping. All ten slept, but what was the difference? The five wise virgins went to sleep being fully prepared. Our symbolic sleeping can be procrastinating our repentance or preparations. Or we may be in willful disobedience (yikes). Whatever the reason, when Christ come again, we must have oil for our lamps. That is the required preparation.

Finally, the announcement is made, “6 And at midnight there was a cry made, Behold, the bridegroom cometh; go ye out to meet him.

7 Then all those virgins arose, and trimmed their lamps.

8 And the foolish said unto the wise, Give us of your oil; for our lamps are gone out.

9 But the wise answered, saying, Not so; lest there be not enough for us and you: but go ye rather to them that sell, and buy for yourselves.”

When we hear that cry we must have oil in our lamps. The time for further preparations has ended. If we don’t have the oil, then we “are left standing in the field”. If we have to purchase oil (make more preparations), the wedding will proceed without us.

“10 And while they went to buy, the bridegroom came; and they that were ready went in with him to the marriage: and the door was shut.

11 Afterward came also the other virgins, saying, Lord, Lord, open to us.

12 But he answered and said, Verily I say unto you, I know you not."

These verses certainly put finality to the situation. One may think that the wise virgins should have helped the foolish ones. I should state that the wise virgins were not being non compassionate. The fact is we cannot live on borrowed light. We have to make our own personal preparations. That is the crux of the meaning of this parsable.

Spencer W. Kimball stated, "This was not selfishness or unkindness. The kind of oil that is needed to illuminate the way and light up the darkness is not shareable. How can one share obedience to the principle of tithing; a mind at peace from righteous living; an accumulation of knowledge? How can one share faith or testimony? How can one share attitudes or chastity.... Each must obtain that kind of oil for himself." (Spencer Kimball, *Faith Precedes the Miracle*, p255, 1972, © Spencer Kimball, Used by Permission of Deseret Book Company.)

The Messiah continues to call out to us, "Come follow me." By doing so we become wise torchbearers.

"13 Watch therefore, for ye know neither the day nor the hour wherein the Son of man cometh."

The Garden of Gethsemane

Mark 14: 26-42

Matthew 26

Luke 22

John 13

It is hard for any humankind happening to be more spiritual than the Last Supper and the proceedings that followed in the Garden of Gethsemane. The garden lies just outside the city's walls. What took place there affects literally every human being, and I for one, am extremely appreciative to the Savior for drinking the bitter cup.

In Jerusalem the time has come for Israel to celebrate the Feast of the Passover. This is a sacred time for Israel and has been practiced for centuries. It is a simple celebration and its meaning relates to the liberation of the Israelites from slavery in Egypt. The timing is always during the month of Nisan on the Hebrew calendar. To our modern day Gregorian calendar that would be in the March/April timeframe. It differs because lunar calendar variations. People celebrate it over conversation and dinner, sometimes telling stories about liberation. I love the family setting of this sacred observance. Often foods that are served during the Passover have symbolic meaning.

There is no universal agreement on the year nor the place where Jesus met with His twelve Apostles in an upper room in a home. Frankly, that is unimportant. What is important is what occurred there. Note, the Lord celebrated the Passover for the Law of Moses had not been fulfilled yet. Per the tradition, an evening meal was served. He was there with His friends. We have not been told all the details of the meal but an exciting element to me is the rite of breaking the bread and serving the water. While the rest of Israel was having their celebratory meals, they partook of foods with symbolic meanings. The introduction of the bread and water also had significance but now in a new way. It was an introduction to the sacrament in which we now celebrate in remembrance of the Savior and His grand gift to us. Let's read now in Mark chapter 14 and absorb its significance.

"22 And as they did eat, Jesus took bread, and blessed, and brake it, and gave to them, and said, Take, eat: this is my body.

23 And he took the cup, and when he had given thanks, he gave it to them: and they all drank of it.

24 And he said unto them, This is my blood of the new testament, which is shed for many."

Having completed that all important new doctrinal ordinance, it was time to move on. "26 And when they had sung an hymn, they went out into the mount of Olives.

Next, Jesus told them several things that were hard for them to understand and accept.

"27 And Jesus saith unto them, All ye shall be offended because of me this night: for it is written, I will smite the shepherd, and the sheep shall be scattered.

28 But after that I am risen, I will go before you into Galilee.

29 But Peter said unto him, Although all shall be offended, yet will not I.

30 And Jesus saith unto him, Verily I say unto thee, That this day, even in this night, before the cock crow twice, thou shalt deny me thrice.

31 But he spake the more vehemently, If I should die with thee, I will not deny thee in any wise. Likewise also said they all."

The holy group walked a little further to the garden. This was not the first time they had been there. I imagine it as a peaceful place and that it provided some solitude, especially during the evening.

"32 And they came to a place which was named Gethsemane: and he saith to his disciples, Sit ye here, while I shall pray.

"33 And he taketh with him Peter and James and John, and began to be sore amazed, and to be very heavy;"

The weight of the sins of the world are beginning to rest of the Christ's shoulders.

"34 And saith unto them, My soul is exceeding sorrowful unto death: tarry ye here, and watch."

Upon arriving at the garden Jesus took only Peter, James, and John with Him as He moved deeper in the garden. That is understandable since they had been designated as the leaders of the Twelve. But then as He proceeds even deeper into the grounds, He wishes to be alone …. for thus it must be so.

"35 And he went forward a little, and fell on the ground, and prayed that, if it were possible, the hour might pass from him.

36 And he said, Abba, Father, all things are possible unto thee; take away this cup from me: nevertheless not what I will, but what thou wilt."

it would be tough to clearly define when the Atonement occurs. Perhaps it is even a process over a long period of time. But certainly the free giving of Himself to the will of our Father in the Garden of Gethsemane was part of the enormous act. I don't think any of us can really understand how it works, but it does! The blessings of that great gift are available unto us all. It is also difficult to comprehend the pain and anguish He suffered. Luke tells us, "And there appeared an angel unto him from heaven, strengthening him." (Luke 22: 43) I would need a legion of angels to get me through a trial like that.

Having physically, emotionally, and spiritually endured the trial, Jesus returns to His trio of trusted disciples. Here is what He finds.

"37 And he cometh, and findeth them sleeping, and saith unto Peter, Simon, sleepest thou? couldest not thou watch one hour?

38 Watch ye and pray, lest ye enter into temptation. The spirit truly is ready, but the flesh is weak."

He could have been talking to me. What a sobering question He asked them. Can I watch for one hour? Can I render service to others consistently? Can I attend my meetings each week? Can I fervently pray to increase my bond with God? The answer to all those questions, and many more, is "absolutely yes", but as the Messiah said, "….the flesh is weak".

The walk back to the three apostles was repeated, with the same results.

"39 And again he went away, and prayed, and spake the same words.

40 And when he returned, he found them asleep again, (for their eyes were heavy,) neither wist they what to answer him."

And once more.

"41 And he cometh the third time, and saith unto them, Sleep on now, and take your rest: it is enough, the hour is come; behold, the Son of man is betrayed into the hands of sinners.

42 Rise up, let us go; lo, he that betrayeth me is at hand."

So my take-away from this lofty teaching is that I have much work left to perform. Perhaps you feel the same way about your life. We must all abandon the ways of the world. We must not follow their forms of entertainment and must not call good bad, and treat bad as good. What we must do is give ourselves to more scripture study, have more fervent declarations of Christ (chapter 6 of this document), find out what lack we yet (chapter 4 of this document), and always submit to the will of the Father and His Son. Say thy will be done, not mine - and mean it. When we hear the invitation, "Come follow me", we should take His hand and follow Him. And keep in mind that the road to celestial glory always goes the through Gethsemane, even for us.

The Intercessory Prayer

John 17

The Apostle John intends that his remarks contained within the chapters of the book ascribed to him to be a narration of the Savior's ministry to those who are already believers. He is not converting, but strengthening. His message is to testify strongly to the truthfulness of the Messiahship and he does so very effectively. In the earlier chapters he is careful to include topics as to who Jesus is with parables of titles that describe Him such as: the True Vine, the Light of the World, the Good Shepherd, plus the Resurrection and the Life.

It is easy to lose track of the timing and location of these events because that is not John's focus. But here is a help. Chapter 13 states that the Twelve are with Christ at the Passover celebration. From that point forward through chapter 17, Jesus is giving last minute instructions to the apostles to bolster their faith in Him and to prepare them for the next couple of days. It is almost like a farewell speech, but that terminology sounds a little less sacred than it should. Upon completion of the instructions, they head to the Garden of Gethsemane. This is another situation where it is useful to our understanding to read certain chapters together in one setting. Chapters 13 - 17 of John are such a case.

Chapter 17 introduces the Intercessory Prayer. When a person acts in an intercessory manner, they are intervening or interceding on behalf of another person. In today's day to day experiences a parent might intercede with a school teacher on behalf of their child. Or an attorney might intervene on behalf of their client in a legal proceeding. I suspect our daily prayers contain examples of intercession for someone. There are of course many other examples, but this chapter relates that God the Son interceded with God the Father in behalf of His apostles …. and then for us. I am blown away by such love and devotion and commitment.

Jesus the Christ began this part of His instructions with a prayer. That is an attentIon getter. I don't wish to break down the Lord's prayer into parts, for the whole chapter is in the tone of intercession. And excessive breaking down and examination may also destroy the spirit and hinder comprehension of the meaning. I don't want this to be a literary discussion, but to be spiritual in nature. But I do want to discuss what we can learn from various verses. The first truth we learn is regarding eternal life and what that means.

"2 As thou hast given him power over all flesh, that he should give eternal to as many as thou hast given him.

3 And this is life eternal, that they might know thee the only true God, and Jesus Christ, whom thou hast sent."

He stated that He has the power to grant all of us eternal life and when we receive eternal life we will individually come to know both God the Father as well the Son. John reiterated this assurance in one of his epistles. "And this is the promise that he hath promised us, even eternal life." (1 John 2:25) But the attainment of eternal life, though a gift from the Messiah, requires us to do our part. Remember the rich young ruler from chapter 4 of this document? The prize is there for our taking.

In verses 6 - 8 Jesus acknowledged to His Father that the men (His apostles) whom the Father blessed Jesus with, have gained an understanding of their roles by having kept the word. They have paid the price for their Apostleship.

"6 I have manifested thy name unto the men which thou gavest me out of the world: thine they were, and thou gavest them me; and they have kept thy word.

7 Now they have known that all things whatsoever thou hast given me are of thee.

8 For I have given unto them the words which thou gavest me; and they have received them, and have known surely that I came out from thee, and they have believed that thou didst send me."

Then He prayed for them. "9 I pray for them: I pray not for the world, but for them which thou hast given me; for they are thine." The Lord knew the huge challenges that awaited their undertaking. He also knew they would need divine guidance and strength to accomplish and endure all things.

Verse 11 contains two holy injunctions. "11 And now I am no more in the world, but these are in the world, and I come to thee. Holy Father, keep through thine own name those whom thou hast given me, that they may be one, as we are." The first is the plea that Heavenly Father "keep" His apostles. This is a simple phrase asking that they will be protected. They will need that blessing to accomplish the rest of their mission. Next, there is the hope that they can be one. That same request is made again by Jesus in verses 22-23. The concept of oneness is important to Christ's church and its direction. Just as in a marriage, effectiveness is enhanced when all are one in purpose.

I think verse 13 might be a surprise to some people. "13 And now come I to thee; and these things I speak in the world, that they might have my joy fulfilled in themselves." Our Savior is asking that they (and I think we) have joy in what we do for Him. Church service and obtaining personal righteousness is not all drudgery and toil. We should find happiness and joy in serving the Lord. This was not a new concept, for Isaiah taught this principle. "Therefore with joy shall ye draw water out of the wells of salvation." (Isaiah 12:3) Having joy with God is a beautiful thought.

There is an old adage in the Christian community. "Be in the world, but not of the world." Perhaps the origin of that expression goes back to John 17: 14-16.

"14 I have given them thy word; and the world hath hated them, because they are not of the world, even as I am not of the world.

15 I pray not that thou shouldest take them out of the world, but that thou shouldest keep them from the evil.

16 They are not of the world, even as I am not of the world."

This is an easy idea to understand. The world is highly influenced by Satan. Following worldly practices in entertainment, appearance, sexual practices, extreme intellectual pursuits, etc, have no place in the Christian church. Jesus is asking for help in keeping them and us free from those entanglements.

Standard dictionaries, such as Merriam-Webster, define *sanctify* as "to set apart to a sacred purpose or to religious use, to free from sin, to impart or impute sacredness, and consecrate". The process of becoming free from sin is accomplished through the Atonement of Jesus Christ. For this reason, Jesus could ask the Father to set His Apostles apart, so that they might complete their mission after He ascends to heaven.

"17 Sanctify them through thy truth: thy word is truth.

19 And for their sakes I sanctify myself, that they also might be sanctified through the truth."

The Messiah doesn't stop there with His sanctification plea. He continues His prayer and asks for same thing for you and I. "20 Neither pray I for these alone, but for them also which shall believe on me through their word;

21 That they all may be one; as thou, Father, art in me, and I in thee, that they also may be one in us: that the world may believe that thou hast sent me."

This is so humbling to me. When I ponder how Jesus went through the pain and anguish in Gethsemane and on Calvary to save me, it helps me to want to be a better person and to follow Him. And then I read that He asked the Father to not only help the apostles obtain oneness with them, but the request went out for me as well.

In Matthew 5:48, we are given the charge to become perfect just as He is. "Be ye therefore perfect, even as your Father which is in heaven is perfect." Our Lord completely understands the enormity of that challenge but He doesn't leave us completely on our own to accomplish it. Next in His prayer the supplication goes to Heaven that divine help be bestowed upon us. “23 I in them, and thou in me, that they may be made perfect in one; and that the world may know that thou hast sent me, and hast loved them, as thou hast loved me.” I am constantly striving daily to allow that prayer to have affect upon me. Then in one day in the future, if I do my part, I may be able to behold their glory. “24 Father, I will that they also, whom thou hast given me, be with me where I am; that they may behold my glory, which thou hast given me: for thou lovedst me before the foundation of the world.”

The benediction of the Intercessory Prayer does not pass without the call for all of us to have the Father’s love within us. “26 And I have declared unto them thy name, and will declare it: that the love wherewith thou hast loved me may be in them, and I in them.” Because of His prayer, the Savior interceded on our behalf, praying to His Father for His Apostles and for all who would believe in Him —including us.

The Good Shepherd

John 10:1-15

Pastoral and agrarian backdrops made excellent scenes for so much of Jesus' teachings. Wheat fields, olive vineyards, fig trees, sheepfolds, lilies, fish, and others were all well known to the people. The usage of them in His parables made it very easy for the people to understand them and to relate to the intended messages. But the rulers and the non-inclined thought they were riddles. The occupation of the shepherd was also well known.

Young David, a paternal ancestor of the Savior himself, was a shepherd. In trying to convince King Saul that he was qualified to go to battle, David related his experience of killing a bear and a lion while protecting his flock. (1 Samuel 17:34-36) So being a shepherd had its hazards. It wasn't just hanging out with and playing with cute little lambs. It couldn't be treated just as a job. It required dedication and courage and eyes had to be focused on the real objective.

I find the shepherding practices to be very interesting. At night time many shepherds banded together and gathered their flocks into one place of safety. The herdsmen took turns watching over the animals during the night to keep away the predators. Then the next morning each individual shepherd came to the portal of the corral and collected just his own sheep. But how could he know exactly which ones were his? After all, they all looked alike. The answer is so simple but yet very amazing. All the shepherds were so close to their sheep and the sheep to them, that a unique call or whistle from the shepherd would be all that was necessary for them to gather around him. These wooly animals would not respond to a counterfeit sound. This is the explanation that the Beloved Apostle provides in chapter 10.

"2 But he that entereth in by the door is the shepherd of the sheep.

3 To him the porter openeth; and the sheep hear his voice: and he calleth his own sheep by name, and leadeth them out.

4 And when he putteth forth his own sheep, he goeth before them, and the sheep follow him: for they know his voice.

5 And a stranger will they not follow, but will flee from him: for they know not the voice of strangers."

But let's go back to verse 1. "Verily, verily, I say unto you, He that entereth not by the door into the sheepfold, but climbeth up some other way, the same is a thief and a robber." This is a parallel learning to the parable of the marriage of the king's son found in Matthew 22. Note what is stated in verses 10-14.

"10 So those servants went out into the highways, and gathered together all as many as they found, both bad and good: and the wedding was furnished with guests.

11 ¶ And when the king came in to see the guests, he saw there a man which had not on a wedding garment:

12 And he saith unto him, Friend, how camest thou in hither not having a wedding garment? And he was speechless.

13 Then said the king to the servants, Bind him hand and foot, and take him away, and cast him into outer darkness; there shall be weeping and gnashing of teeth.

14 For many are called, but few are chosen."

There was a special protocol for invited guests. Gate crashers were easily recognized and prohibited from entering. Likewise, if a person tried to enter the sheepfold in an improper manner, he was denied. My lesson learned here is that the Lord has a straight and narrow path for us to follow to return to the fold (Him). I need to follow the prescribed order: acceptance of Christ, baptism, obedience, service, forgiveness, loving, etc. Yes, there are more steps, plenty more, and they all bring me happiness. I need to follow the Good Shepherd. Fortunately, John recorded this parable in chapter 10 for us to have and learn from.

“7 Then said Jesus unto them again, Verily, verily, I say unto you, I am the door of the sheep.

8 All that ever came before me are thieves and robbers: but the sheep did not hear them.

9 I am the door: by me if any man enter in, he shall be saved, and shall go in and out, and find pasture.”

Again He tells us that safe entry into His pasture is through Him - the door.

The ways of the world are workings of Satan and are represented here as thieves. “10 The thief cometh not, but for to steal, and to kill, and to destroy: I am come that they might have life, and that they might have it more abundantly.”

The workings of the atonement and the sacrifice of the Christ brings to pass our eternal life. “11 I am the good shepherd: the good shepherd giveth his life for the sheep.”

Near the beginning of this chapter I stated that an effective shepherd can’t treat his responsibilities as a mere posting. When he does, this is what happens. “12 But he that is an hireling, and not the shepherd, whose own the sheep are not, seeth the wolf coming, and leaveth the sheep, and fleeth: and the wolf catcheth them, and scattereth the sheep.

13 The hireling fleeth, because he is an hireling, and careth not for the sheep."

14 I am the good shepherd, and know my sheep, and am known of mine.

15 As the Father knoweth me, even so know I the Father: and I lay down my life for the sheep."

I am so grateful that Jesus of Nazareth laid down His life for me, a mere little lamb. I want to always be able to recognize His voice and to follow His ways. Sheep prefer to be led. I want to be led by the Messiah and the Good Shepherd.

A powerful personal story told to me by a friend years ago comes to mind that supports this parable. This friend was serving as a Bishop and one night he returned home very late after handling church business at the end of his work day. In fact, he was so exhausted that he skipped dinner and went to bed. After about 30 minutes, his phone rang. He answered the call with the usual "Hello". The person on the other end of the line began the conversation without announcing who he was said, "Bishop, I have a problem." The man went on to explain that he had been asked to serve a mission but he was very unsure of what he should do and he wanted some advice. My friend was a little bewildered because he didn't know who he was speaking with. So he simply asked, "I'm sorry, who is this?" The reply was completely surprising to him. The man said, “What? This is your father!” My friend lamented that he didn’t recognize the voice of his own father. We should be in tune to always recognize the voice of our Heavenly Father.

Bibliography

Kimball, Spencer W. "Fatih Precedes the Miracle." GospeLink Digital Library, 2022. 7 September 2022. <https://www.gospelink.com/library/contents/113>

Lund, Gerald N. "Selected Writings Of Gerald N. Lund: Gospel Scholars Series." GospeLink Digital Library, 2022. 5 September 2022. <https://www.gospelink.com/library/contents/621>

Metaxas, Eric. "Bonhoeffer, Pastor, Martyr, Prophet, Spy." Nashville: Thomas Nelson, 2010.

"sanctify." *Merriam-Webster.com*. Merriam-Webster, 2022. Web. 10 September 2022.

www.ingramcontent.com/pod-product-compliance
Lightning Source LLC
LaVergne TN
LVHW052053160826
845678LV00015B/3206

9798362371128